50 WAYS WITH

VEGETABLES

50 WAYS WITH
VEGETABLES

ROSEMARY WADEY

LITTLE BROWN
AND COMPANY
BOSTON • TORONTO • LONDON

A Little, Brown Book

Little, Brown and Company (UK) Ltd
Brettenham House, Lancaster Place, London WC2E 7EN

First published in 1991
First published in the UK by Little, Brown and Company in 1993
Reprinted in 1997

© Copyright: Lansdowne Publishing Pty Ltd 1991
© Copyright design: Lansdowne Publishing Pty Ltd 1991

Lansdowne Publishing Pty Ltd
Level 1, Argyle Centre, 18 Argyle Street, The Rocks, Sydney NSW 2000, Australia

ISBN: 0 316 90601 8

A CIP catalogue record for this book is available from
the British Library

Designed by Kathie Baxter Smith
Photography by Andrew Elton
Food Styling by Mary Harris
Recipes typeset in Granjon by Character, North Sydney
Printed in Singapore by Tien Wah Press (Pte) Ltd

Front cover photograph: Hot Potato Salad, recipe page 60
page 2: Green and Gold Vegetable Medley, recipe page 56
Pages 8 & 9: Zucchini and Tarragon Quiches, recipe page 106
Back cover photograph: Potato Galette with Chives, recipe page 76

CONTENTS

Introduction 6
The Recipes 9

INTRODUCTION

Vegetables have come into their own as highly valued ingredients in the principal meal of the day. In the diet of many individuals and families, they now take pride of place. This book reflects the increased interest in these delightfully varied foods, and the numerous tempting ways in which they can be prepared, to provide starters, main courses, accompaniments and even desserts.

Vegetables are ideal ingredients in light and healthy meals: they are not only full of nutrients, quick to prepare and easy to eat, but they are also among the most colorful and decorative items in the world of good food.

Vegetables are essential in every diet: they are high in many vitamins, especially vitamins A, B and C, as well as being sources of minerals such as calcium and iron. They also contain fiber, which we can benefit from by cooking and eating them with their skins on.

An enormous selection of vegetables is available, freshly displayed each day in greengrocers' stores and supermarkets. Any prepacked goods will have both a sell-by and a use-by date marked on the package, to ensure that we buy fresh items. Other good sources of fresh vegetables are the many open markets and stalls which can be found in towns, villages, farm shops or beside the road in rural areas. Although fresh produce is always preferable, frozen and canned vegetables ensure that out-of-season varieties are widely available all year round.

Always select the freshest vegetables: cheaper produce is not worth considering if it is limp and inferior, because this will mean wastage in preparation, and a poor flavor that no amount of cooking will enhance.

Buy little and often when it comes to vegetables, and do not store them for too long. Root vegetables will stay fresh for five to six days if kept in a cool, dry, well-ventilated place, preferably in a rack to ensure air circulation. Green vegetables are best used within three days, and Swiss chard or spinach should be eaten within twenty-four hours. Plastic bags and plastic wrap (cling film) should not be used for storage unless large holes are made for ventilation. Paper bags are best, as they do not cause sweating, and the net bags in which some vegetables are prepacked are also suitable for storage. Green vegetables and all salad ingredients must be kept in a cool place: a special cooler drawer or the bottom shelf of your refrigerator are ideal.

When preparing vegetables, leave the skins on if possible and simply wash thoroughly or scrub. If peeling is necessary, take care to do this thinly, as valuable nutrients are found just under the skin.

Cooking methods are important. Do not overcook vegetables, as they become unattractive and tasteless, and lose their nutritive value. Cooked vegetables should still have a slight 'bite' to them. To achieve this effect, it is best to steam them, or cook them in a microwave oven: either of these methods tends to conserve the nutrients contained in the food. Other methods of cooking are baking, braising, frying, roasting and boiling. The recipes in this book give the appropriate times for each, to guarantee the freshness and lightness of each dish.

When fresh vegetables are plentiful, it is a good idea to home-freeze some for future use. They usually need blanching after preparation to achieve the best results, and can then be stored in a freezer for six to nine months. Remember to use the 'fast freeze' section of your freezer for the actual freezing process. Many cooked vegetable dishes can also be frozen for use at a later date. These are usually best thawed before recooking in a conventional or microwave oven. Plain frozen vegetables, on the other hand, cook more quickly and taste better if they are recooked from the frozen state.

Vegetables can be served as a main meal in their own right, as part of a meal, or as snacks and starters. A main vegetable can be combined with others, rice or pasta, to create very interesting dishes. Sauces give variety and flavor, and many people who add an exciting sauce to an old favourite will find they have created a new dish for their personal collection. Cheese, meat, fish, poultry and eggs can all be combined with vegetables in imaginative ways, as recipes in this book demonstrate.

For weight-watchers, vegetarians, those who like to entertain at home, or people who simply like appetizing meals that delight the eye, this book provides a fascinating range for all tastes and occasions.

THE RECIPES

ARTICHOKE HEARTS PROVENÇALE

2 × 15 oz (425 g) cans artichoke
   hearts, drained
12 baby onions, peeled
2 tablespoons vegetable oil
1 clove garlic, crushed
4 large tomatoes, peeled and
   quartered
1 level tablespoon tomato paste
   (purée)
4 tablespoons white wine
12 black olives
2 tablespoons lemon juice
1 tablespoon capers
chopped parsley or coriander to
   garnish

Halve the artichokes and lay them in a lightly greased ovenproof casserole. In a pan fry the onions in the oil until beginning to brown, stirring frequently then transfer them to the casserole.

Add the garlic, tomatoes, tomato paste and wine to the pan and bring to the boil. Simmer for 2 to 3 minutes then add the olives, lemon juice, capers and seasonings.

Pour over the artichokes, cover and cook in a moderate oven (350°F, 180°C, Gas Mark 4) for 30 to 40 minutes. Alternatively, place in a microwave and cook on MAXIMUM (100%) for 6 minutes.

Serve hot or cold liberally sprinkled with chopped parsley or coriander.

Preparation time about 20 minutes
Cooking time about 30 minutes
Serves 4 to 6

AVIYAL CURRY

8 oz (250 g) shredded (desiccated)
    coconut
1¼ cups (½ pint, 300 ml) water
¼ cup (2 oz, 50 g) butter or
    margarine
1 oz (25 g) fresh ginger, peeled and
    finely chopped
3 cloves garlic, crushed
2 onions, peeled and chopped
2 level teaspoons ground coriander
1 level tablespoon garam masala
1 level teaspoon turmeric
1 level teaspoon salt
8 oz (250 g) broccoli, cut into
    small florets
2 green bell peppers (capsicums),
    seeded and sliced
8 oz (250 g) carrots, peeled and
    sliced
4–6 oz (100–175 g) green beans,
    trimmed and halved or
    quartered
1 green chili, seeded and finely
    chopped
freshly chopped coriander or
    parsley

Purée the coconut and water in a food processor or blender until smooth.

Heat the butter in a heavy based pan, add the ginger and garlic and fry for a few minutes. Add the onions and continue cooking until they are golden brown, stirring from time to time.

Add the coriander, garam masala, turmeric and salt and simmer for 2 to 3 minutes then add the vegetables and chili and continue to cook gently for 3 to 4 minutes, giving a good stir.

Add the coconut purée and bring the mixture to the boil. Cover and simmer for about 10 minutes. Alternatively, place in a microwave on MAXIMUM (100%) for 3 to 4 minutes, stirring once.

Adjust the seasonings and serve sprinkled liberally with coriander or parsley.

Preparation time about 20 minutes
Cooking time about 25 minutes
Serves 4 to 6

BAIGAN TAMATAR
SPICY VEGETABLES

2 onions, peeled and chopped
3 oz (75 g) butter or margarine
1 clove garlic, crushed
½ level teaspoon chili powder
1 bay leaf
1 inch (2.5 cm) piece cinnamon
  stick
salt and pepper
3 tablespoons water
1 lb (500 g) tomatoes, peeled and
  quartered
1 lb (500 g) eggplants
  (aubergines), trimmed and
  diced
2 level tablespoons tomato paste
  (purée)
chopped parsley to garnish

Fry the onions in the melted butter gently for about 10 minutes, then add the garlic, chili powder, bay leaf, cinnamon stick and seasonings and continue cooking for 2 to 3 minutes, stirring all the time.

Add the water and tomatoes and simmer gently for 5 minutes. Add the eggplants and tomato paste, cover and simmer very gently for 20 to 30 minutes, stirring from time to time until the eggplants are tender but not too broken up. Alternatively, place in a microwave on MAXIMUM (100%) for 3 minutes; stir and cook a further 3 to 4 minutes.

Adjust seasonings and serve sprinkled with parsley.

Preparation time about 20 minutes
Cooking time about 40 minutes
Serves 4 to 5

BAKED MUSHROOMS

8 large flat mushrooms or large
 open-cup mushrooms
vegetable oil
6 oz (175 g) chopped cooked Swiss
 chard (spinach)
2 oz (50 g) salami, garlic sausage
 or cooked ham, finely chopped
2 oz (50 g) cream cheese or cottage
 cheese
salt and pepper
good pinch of ground coriander or
 nutmeg
1 egg yolk
1 level tablespoon grated parmesan
 cheese
1½–2 oz (40–50 g) blue cheese,
 crumbled
1 oz (25 g) fresh breadcrumbs

Trim and wipe the mushrooms and brush lightly all over with oil. Stand in an ovenproof dish.

Combine the Swiss chard (spinach), salami, sausage or ham, cream or cottage cheese, seasonings, coriander or nutmeg and egg yolk. Divide between the mushrooms, pressing the stuffing evenly around the stalk.

Combine the parmesan, blue cheese and breadcrumbs and sprinkle over the filled mushrooms.

Cook uncovered in a fairly hot oven (400°F, 200°C, Gas Mark 6) for about 20 minutes. Serve hot.

Preparation time about 20 minutes
Cooking time about 20 minutes
Serves 4

BAKED POTATOES WITH STILTON

4 large baking potatoes (approx 12 oz, 350 g each)
2 tablespoons (1 oz, 25 g) butter or margarine
1 level tablespoon freshly snipped chives
1 level tablespoon freshly chopped thyme or marjoram
salt and pepper
2 tablespoons milk
6 oz (175 g) Stilton cheese, crumbled or coarsely grated

Scrub the potatoes and prick all over. Cook in a hot oven (425°F, 220°C, Gas Mark 7) for 1–1 1/4 hours or until tender. Alternatively, place pricked potatoes on a paper towel in a microwave on HIGH (100%) for 6 minutes; turn and cook for 7 minutes; then cook filled potatoes for 2 to 3 minutes.

Cut the tops off each potato and carefully scoop out most of the flesh. Mash the flesh and then beat in the butter, chives, thyme or marjoram, seasonings and milk. Finally beat in 4 oz (100 g) of the cheese.

Spoon the potato filling back into the skins, piling it up as necessary. Stand on a baking sheet and sprinkle with the remaining cheese. Return to the oven for about 10 to 15 minutes or place under a moderate broiler (grill) for a few minutes until golden brown.

Serve garnished with salads and fresh herbs or use as an accompaniment to another dish.

Preparation time about 15 minutes
Cooking time about 1 1/2 hours
Serves 4

Variations: Replace the blue cheese with grated cheddar, gouda, gruyère or cottage cheese and alter the herbs to suit your choice and availability. Other additions such as chopped cooked bacon or ham, salami, chopped tomatoes or fried mushrooms can also be added.

BOSTON BAKED BEANS

12 oz (350 g) dried haricot beans
2 tablespoons treacle (molasses)
2 level tablespoons tomato paste
  (purée)
1 level tablespoon dry mustard
2 level teaspoons salt
freshly ground black pepper
½ teaspoon Worcestershire sauce
2 tablespoons wine vinegar
1 level tablespoon demerara sugar
2 onions, peeled and chopped
1–2 cloves garlic, crushed
6–8 whole cloves
8–12 oz (250–350 g) belly pork
  slices, skinned and diced or 8 oz
  (250 g) button mushrooms,
  trimmed
freshly chopped parsley or mixed
  herbs

Wash the beans thoroughly then soak overnight in cold water. Drain the beans, put into a pan and cover with fresh cold water. Bring to the boil and simmer for 30 minutes. Drain and reserve the liquid.

Place the beans in a heavy casserole and stir in the treacle, tomato paste, mustard, seasonings, Worcestershire sauce, vinegar, sugar, onions, garlic and cloves. Add the pork, if used, and pour in about 2 cups (16 fl oz, 500 ml) of the cooking liquid made up with water if necessary.

Mix well and cover the casserole tightly. Cook in a slow oven (300°F, 150°C, Gas Mark 2) for 7 to 8 hours. If using mushrooms, add an hour before the end of cooking.

Discard the cloves, give the casserole a good stir and serve sprinkled with parsley or herbs and with plenty of crusty bread.

Preparation time about 20 minutes plus soaking
Cooking time 7–8 hours
Serves 4

Note: This dish needs long slow cooking, but it is ideal to cook while you are out at work, or even overnight; it can be reheated gently when required.

BRAISED FENNEL WITH ORANGE

4 small bulbs or 2 very large
    bulbs fennel
3 oranges
1½ cups (12 fl oz, 350 ml) stock
2 tablespoons (1 oz, 25 g) butter or
    margarine
1 oz (25 g) flour
salt and pepper
2 level tablespoons toasted chopped
    hazelnuts or almonds

Trim the fennel, cutting off the bases and any feathery fronds. Chop the fronds and reserve for garnish. Cut the fennel bulbs in half and place in a pan. Thinly pare the rind from one orange free of white pith and cut into julienne strips. Squeeze the juice from 2 oranges.

Add the orange juice and stock to the fennel, bring to the boil and simmer gently for about 15 minutes. Add the strips of orange rind and continue to cook for 5 to 6 minutes until just tender. Drain and arrange the fennel in a serving dish with orange strips, reserving the cooking liquid. Cut away the peel and white pith from the remaining orange and ease out the segments.

Blend the butter and flour together until smooth and gradually beat into the cooking juices, a small knob at a time. Bring back to the boil, cooking until thickened and smooth.

Add the orange segments and seasonings to taste to the sauce, simmer for about a minute then pour over the fennel.

Before serving, sprinkle over all with the reserved chopped fennel fronds and hazelnuts or almonds.

Preparation time about 20 minutes
Cooking time 25 minutes
Serves 4

BROCCOLI AND
BLUE CHEESE QUICHE

1½ cups (6 oz, 175 g) malted
    wheat flour
pinch of salt
3 tablespoons (1½ oz, 40 g) butter
    or margarine
3 tablespoons (1½ oz, 40 g) white
    fat or lard
cold water to mix
12 oz (350 g) broccoli
salt and pepper
1 level tablespoon snipped chives
6 oz (175 g) crumbly blue cheese
    (Stilton, Danish blue, blue
    Shropshire etc.)
3 eggs
¾ cup (6 fl oz, 175 ml) milk
½ cup (4 fl oz, 125 ml) natural
    yogurt
6–8 oz (175–250 g) carrots, peeled
    and cut into thin sticks

Put the flour and salt into a bowl, rub in the butter and lard until the mixture resembles fine breadcrumbs. Add sufficient water to mix to a pliable dough. Roll out the pastry and use to line an 8 inch (20 cm) tart pan (flan dish), crimp the edge and chill.

Trim the broccoli and cook in boiling salted water for 5 minutes. Drain, cool and chop roughly. Place the broccoli in the tart case and sprinkle with the chives. Crumble the cheese (or coarsely grate) and lay over the vegetables. Beat the eggs with the milk and yogurt until quite smooth, season well and pour over the cheese.

Cook in a fairly hot oven (400°F, 200°C, Gas Mark 6) for about 40 to 45 minutes until well risen, golden brown and firm to the touch.

Meanwhile cook the carrots in boiling water until tender crisp; drain well and keep warm.

When the quiche is ready arrange the carrot sticks around the top edge of it and serve at once. It can also be served cold.

Preparation time 20 to 25 minutes
Cooking time about 45 minutes
Serves 4 to 6

BROCCOLI AND CHEESE SOUFFLÉ

8 oz (250 g) broccoli
4 oz (100 g) mushrooms, chopped
    or sliced
1 tablespoon vegetable oil
2 tablespoons (1 oz, 25 g) butter or
    margarine
1 oz (25 g) flour
⅔ cup (¼ pint, 150 ml) milk
salt and pepper
½ level teaspoon prepared English
    mustard
½ level teaspoon Dijon mustard
3 oz (75 g) mature cheddar cheese,
    finely grated
2 level tablespoons grated
    parmesan cheese
3–4 eggs, separated

Cut the broccoli into florets and cook in boiling water for 2 to 3 minutes, then drain and chop roughly.

Fry the mushrooms briefly in the oil until just cooked. Drain.

Grease an 8 inch (20 cm) soufflé dish and place the cooked broccoli and mushrooms in the base.

Melt the butter in a pan, stir in the flour and cook for a minute or two, stirring continuously. Bring to the boil. Remove from the heat and beat in the seasonings, mustard and cheeses followed by the egg yolks, one at a time. Beat the egg whites until very stiff and standing in peaks. Beat 2 tablespoons of the egg white into the sauce and quickly fold in the remainder evenly.

Pour at once into the soufflé dish over the vegetables and cook in a fairly hot oven (400°F, 200°C, Gas Mark 6) for 35 to 40 minutes until well risen and browned. Do not be tempted to look in the oven for the first 30 minutes of cooking or the soufflé will sink, and when you do look, close the door very carefully for a blast of cool air or a sudden jolt can also cause it to sink. Serve immediately.

Preparation time about 30 minutes
Cooking time about 40 minutes
Serves 4

CABBAGE DOLMAS

4 oz (100 g) cooked rice
2–3 scallions (green onions, spring onions) trimmed and chopped
2 oz (50 g) chopped hazelnuts
½ small red bell pepper (capsicum), seeded and finely chopped
2 oz (50 g) mushrooms, finely chopped
salt and pepper
½ level teaspoon dried mixed herbs
¼ level teaspoon ground coriander
1 egg, beaten
1 cup (8 fl oz, 250 ml) stock (vegetables or chicken)
approx ¾ cup (¼ pint, 150 ml) milk or skimmed milk
2 level teaspoons cornstarch (cornflour)
8–12 large green cabbage leaves

Put the rice into a bowl and mix in the scallions, hazelnuts, red bell pepper and mushrooms. Add seasonings, herbs and coriander, mix well and bind with the egg.

Trim the tough base stem from each cabbage leaf and blanch leaves in boiling water for 2 minutes. Drain well. Put a spoonful of the stuffing at the stem end of each leaf, fold in the edges and roll up to completely enclose the filling. Place in a pan in a single layer.

Pour the stock onto the dolmas, bring to the boil, and simmer gently for 15 minutes. Alternatively, place in a microwave on MAXIMUM (100%) and cook for 5 to 7 minutes.

Transfer the dolmas to a serving dish and keep warm. Make the cooking juices up to 1¼ cups (½ pint, 300 ml) with the milk, return to the pan and thicken with the cornstarch blended in a little of the milk. Bring back to the boil until thickened, season to taste and pour over the dolmas.

Preparation time about 20 minutes
Cooking time about 20 minutes
Serves 4

CARAWAY CABBAGE

2 lb (1 kg) white cabbage,
    trimmed
1 cup (8 fl oz, 250 ml) milk or
    skimmed milk
salt and coarsely ground black
    pepper
⅔ cup (4 oz, 100 g) raisins
1 level teaspoon caraway seeds
    (optional)
freshly chopped mint to garnish

Remove the hard core from the cabbage and shred finely and evenly. Put into a pan with the milk and bring to the boil. Cover and simmer very gently for about 15 minutes, giving an occasional stir.

Season the cabbage with a little salt and plenty of coarse black pepper. Add the raisins and caraway seeds. Continue to cook gently in a covered pan, for 5 minutes. The cabbage is best served still with a 'bite' in it but can be cooked longer until quite tender if preferred. Alternatively, place in a microwave on MAXIMUM (100%) for 4 minutes; stir well and cook a further 4 minutes, then stir in raisins and caraway seeds and cook for 1 to 2 minutes.

Drain off the excess milk before serving, turn into a dish and sprinkle liberally with freshly chopped mint.

Preparation time 10 minutes
Cooking time about 20 minutes
Serves 4

Variations: Milk may be replaced with stock, if preferred. Add 2 to 4 tablespoons finely chopped salami, garlic sausage or bacon if desired; or toss with 8 oz (250 g) cooked carrot sticks just before serving.

CARROT AND TARRAGON LASAGNE

8 sheets green lasagne
salt and pepper
3 tablespoons vegetable oil
1 large onion, peeled and thinly
  sliced
1 clove garlic, crushed
12 oz (350 g) carrots, peeled and
  chopped
2 sticks celery, sliced
6 oz (175 g) button mushrooms,
  quartered
15 oz (425 g) can peeled tomatoes
1 level tablespoon tomato paste
  (purée)
good dash of Worcestershire sauce
1 level tablespoon freshly chopped
  tarragon or 1 level teaspoon
  dried tarragon
3 tablespoons (1½ oz, 40 g)
  butter or margarine
⅓ cup (1½ oz, 40 g) flour
2 cups (16 fl oz, 475 ml) milk
1 level teaspoon dry mustard
2 oz (50 g) mature cheddar cheese,
  grated
2 hard-cooked eggs, sliced
2 level tablespoons grated
  parmesan cheese
2 level tablespoons dried
  breadcrumbs

Cook the lasagne, a few sheets at a time, in boiling salted water with 1 tablespoon oil added, until tender, then drain. (Check whether your lasagne needs pre-cooking, some varieties do not.)

Heat the remaining oil and fry the onion, garlic, carrots and celery for 5 to 6 minutes until beginning to soften. Add the mushrooms, tomatoes and their juice, tomato paste, Worcestershire sauce, tarragon and seasonings and bring to the boil. Cover and simmer for 5 to 6 minutes.

Melt the butter in a pan, stir in the flour and cook for a minute or so. Gradually add the milk and bring to the boil. Season well, add the mustard and simmer for 2 minutes; then stir in the cheddar until melted.

Layer up the lasagne in a greased ovenproof dish with the vegetable mixture and most of the sauce. Arrange the sliced eggs on top then cover with the remaining sauce. Sprinkle with the parmesan and breadcrumbs and cook in a fairly hot oven (400°F, 200°C, Gas Mark 6) for 30 to 40 minutes until brown and bubbling. Alternatively, place in a microwave to cook or reheat on MAXIMUM (100%) for 5 minutes.

Preparation time about 40 minutes
Cooking time about 45 minutes
Serves 4 to 5

CARROT NUTBURGERS

1 onion, peeled and chopped
1 clove garlic, crushed
2 tablespoons (1 oz) butter or margarine
¼ cup (1 oz, 25 g) flour
½ cup (4 fl oz, 125 ml) vegetable stock
2 cups (8 oz, 250 g) mixed chopped nuts
2 oz (50 g) fresh breadcrumbs, brown or white
2 carrots, peeled and coarsely grated
1 level tablespoon freshly chopped parsley
1 level teaspoon dried thyme
1 tablespoon lemon juice
salt and pepper
1 level teaspoon vegetable extract

Fry the onion and garlic in the butter until soft, but not colored. Stir in the flour and cook for a minute or so.

Gradually add the stock and bring to the boil. Remove from the heat and stir in the nuts, breadcrumbs, carrots, parsley, thyme, lemon juice, seasonings and vegetable extract; let stand until cold.

Divide the mixture into four and shape into round burgers or cutlet shapes and place on a greased baking sheet.

Cook in a moderate oven (350°F, 180°C, Gas Mark 4) for about 25 minutes or until lightly browned and crisp. Serve hot or cold garnished with salads.

Preparation time about 20 minutes
Cooking time about 30 minutes
Serves 4

CELERIAC PUREE WITH CARROTS

1½ lb (750 g) celeriac
salt and pepper
½ lb (250 g) carrots, peeled and
*   coarsely grated*
2 tablespoons (1 oz, 25 g) butter or
*   margarine*
3 tablespoons low fat natural
*   yogurt or low fat fromage frais*
freshly chopped parsley

Peel the celeriac carefully, then chop roughly and cook in boiling salted water until tender, about 20 minutes.

Meanwhile cook the carrots in boiling water for 3 to 4 minutes.

Drain the celeriac and mash thoroughly or purée in a food processor. Season well and beat in the butter and yogurt.

Drain the carrots thoroughly and fold through the celeriac purée. If desired also beat in 1 to 2 tablespoons freshly chopped parsley (not dried parsley). Turn into a serving dish and sprinkle liberally with parsley.

Preparation time about 15 minutes
Cooking time about 25 minutes
Serves 4 to 6

CHEESE, ONION AND ANCHOVY FLAN

1½ cups (6 oz, 175 g) flour
pinch of salt
3 tablespoons (1½ oz, 40 g) lard
3 tablespoons (1½ oz, 40 g)
  butter or margarine
cold water to mix
1 lb (500 g) onions, peeled and
  thinly sliced
1 clove garlic, crushed (optional)
2 tablespoons vegetable oil
6 oz (175 g) mature cheddar
  cheese, grated
2 eggs, beaten
⅔ cup (¼ pint, 150 ml) light
  (single) cream or milk
salt and pepper
1 can anchovy fillets, drained
black olives
parsley

Sift the flour and salt into a bowl and rub in the butter and lard until the mixture resembles fine breadcrumbs. Add sufficient cold water to mix to a pliable dough. Wrap in polythene or foil and chill while preparing the filling.

Fry the onions and garlic in the oil very gently for about 15 to 20 minutes until very soft but only just beginning to color, stirring well from time to time. Let stand to cool.

Roll out the pastry and use to line an 8 inch (20 cm) tart pan (flan dish). Spread the onions over the base and then sprinkle with the cheese.

Beat the eggs, cream and seasonings together and pour over the cheese. Cook in a hot oven (425°F, 220°C, Gas Mark 7) for 20 minutes. Lay the anchovy fillets over the custard filling, reduce the oven temperature to moderate (350°F, 180°C, Gas Mark 4) and continue for 20 to 25 minutes until lightly browned and cooked through.

Serve hot or cold garnished with black olives and parsley.

Preparation time about 30 minutes
Cooking time about 45 minutes
Serves 4 to 5

CHILI BEAN HOTPOT

2 onions, peeled and sliced
1–2 cloves garlic, crushed
2 tablespoons vegetable oil
6–8 sticks celery, sliced
1 red bell pepper (capsicum),
   seeded and sliced
½–1 small green chili pepper,
   seeded and finely chopped
   (optional)
15 oz (425 g) can tomatoes
1 level tablespoon tomato paste
   (purée)
1–2 level teaspoons mild chili
   powder
salt and pepper
⅓ cup (¼ pint, 150 ml) vegetable
   stock
15 oz (425 g) can red kidney or
   cannelini beans, drained
1½–2 lb (750 g–1 kg) potatoes,
   parboiled
little melted butter
chopped parsley to garnish

Fry the onions and garlic gently in the oil until soft. Add the celery, bell pepper and chili and cook for a few minutes longer.

Add the tomatoes, tomato paste, chili powder, seasonings, stock and beans and simmer for 4 to 5 minutes.

Turn the vegetables into an ovenproof casserole. Slice the potatoes and arrange over the vegetables. Brush with melted butter and cook in a fairly hot oven (400°F, 200°C, Gas Mark 6) for 1¼ to 1½ hours until golden brown. Serve sprinkled with parsley.

Preparation time about 20 minutes
Cooking time about 1¼ to 1½ hours
Serves 4

CREAMED BRUSSELS SPROUTS WITH CHESTNUTS

1½–2 lb (750 g–1 kg) Brussels
    sprouts, trimmed
salt and pepper
2 tablespoons (1 oz, 25 g) butter or
    margarine
¼ cup (1 oz, 25 g) flour
¾ cup (6 fl oz, 175 ml) light
    (single) cream or milk
good pinch of ground nutmeg
1 tablespoon wine vinegar
4–6 oz (100–175 g) chestnuts,
    roasted or boiled

Cook the sprouts in boiling salted water until just tender, about 5 to 8 minutes, then drain very thoroughly.

Meanwhile melt the butter in a pan, stir in the flour and cook for a minute or so. Gradually add the cream and bring to the boil, stirring from time to time; simmer only very gently for about a minute. Stir in the nutmeg and vinegar and season to taste.

Finely chop or purée the drained sprouts and mix with the white sauce. Turn into a serving dish and sprinkle with the roughly chopped chestnuts.

Preparation time about 15 minutes
Cooking time about 15 minutes
Serves 4 to 6

CRISPY MUSHROOMS WITH TARRAGON AND PEPPER DIP

16–20 closed cup mushrooms
1 egg, beaten
dried or golden breadcrumbs
½ cup (4 fl oz, 100 ml) low fat
  fromage frais
2 level tablespoons low calorie
  mayonnaise
1 hard-cooked egg, finely grated
1 level tablespoon freshly chopped
  tarragon or 1 level teaspoon
  dried tarragon, crumbled
¼ small red bell pepper
  (capsicum), seeded and very
  finely chopped
1 clove garlic, crushed
salt and pepper
shredded lettuce
raddichio

Trim off the mushroom stalks level with the base, then dip each mushroom in beaten egg and then coat thoroughly in breadcrumbs.

Stand each mushroom stalk-side downwards, on a lightly greased baking sheet. Cook in a hot oven (425°F, 220°C, Gas Mark 7) for about 20 minutes until crisp and cooked through.

While the mushrooms are cooking, make the dip: beat the fromage frais and mayonnaise together until smooth then beat in the grated egg, tarragon, red bell pepper and garlic until smooth; season to taste.

Serve the mushrooms hot on individual plates on shredded lettuce, garnished with raddichio leaves and with a large spoonful of the sauce on each plate. Serve the rest of the sauce separately.

Preparation time about 15 minutes
Cooking time about 20 minutes
Serves 4

Deep-fried Stuffed Mushrooms

12–16 open cup mushrooms
    (approx 8 oz, 250 g) trimmed
¾ cup (6 oz, 175 g) cream cheese
salt and pepper
1 clove garlic, crushed
1 level tablespoon chopped chives
1 level tablespoon freshly chopped
    mint
1 egg, beaten
golden or dried breadcrumbs
vegetable oil
6 tablespoons thick mayonnaise
2 tablespoons natural yogurt
2 level tablespoons freshly chopped
    mint (extra)

Trim the stalks of the mushrooms almost flat and wipe all over.

Combine the cream cheese, seasonings, garlic, chives and mint and spread into the 'hollow' in the mushrooms around the stalk.

Dip each mushroom into beaten egg and then coat thoroughly in breadcrumbs; chill until ready to cook.

Blend mayonnaise, yogurt and extra mint in a blender or food processor until a pale green. Turn into a bowl. Heat the oil until a cube of bread browns in 30 seconds. Fry the mushrooms about 6 at a time until golden brown and crisp. Drain on paper towels and keep warm while frying the remainder.

Serve hot garnished with a salad, lemon wedges and with the mayonnaise.

Preparation time about 20 minutes
Cooking time about 10 minutes
Serves 4

EGGPLANT RATATOUILLE

1 large onion, peeled and sliced
1–2 cloves garlic, crushed
2 tablespoons vegetable oil
1 each red, yellow and green bell
    pepper (capsicum), seeded and
    sliced
12 oz (350 g) eggplant
    (aubergine), halved lengthwise
    and sliced
12 oz (350 g) zucchini
    (courgettes), trimmed and cut
    into sticks
4 large tomatoes, peeled and sliced
1 level tablespoon tomato paste
    (purée)
2 tablespoons water or stock
salt and black pepper
½ level teaspoon dried thyme
    (optional)
3 slices bread, brown or white
vegetable oil
freshly chopped parsley

Fry the onion and garlic in the oil in a flameproof casserole until soft.

Add the bell peppers and cook for 2 to 4 minutes, stirring frequently.

Stir in the eggplant, zucchini and tomatoes and mix well. Blend the tomato paste with the water or stock and add to the casserole with plenty of seasonings and the thyme (if used).

Bring to the boil, cover the casserole and cook in a moderate oven (350°F, 180°C, Gas Mark 4) for about 40 minutes. Alternatively, cover and place in a microwave on MAXIMUM (100%) for 5 minutes; stir and cook a further 3 to 4 minutes.

Make the bread croutons by removing the crusts and cutting slices into triangles. Fry in shallow oil until golden and drain. Dip in chopped parsley.

Adjust the seasonings of the ratatouille and serve surrounded with parsley croutons.

Preparation time 15 minutes
Cooking time about 40 minutes
Serves 4

ELIZABETHAN PIE

2 cups (8 oz, 250 g) flour
pinch of salt
¼ cup (2 oz, 50 g) butter or
  margarine
¼ cup (2 oz, 50 g) lard
cold water to mix
¾–1 lb (350–500 g) Jerusalem
  artichokes
1 onion, peeled and chopped
2 tablespoons (1 oz, 25 g) butter or
  margarine (extra), melted
4 oz (100 g) white grapes, halved
  and pipped
2 oz (50 g) stoned dates, chopped
2 hard-cooked eggs, sliced
salt and pepper
1 level teaspoon mixed herbs
beaten egg or milk to glaze
4–6 tablespoons light (single)
  cream or natural yogurt

Make the pastry by sifting the flour with the salt and rubbing in the butter and lard until the mixture resembles fine breadcrumbs. Add sufficient water to mix to a pliable dough, wrap and chill.

Peel the artichokes and plunge them immediately into salted water, or water with a dash of lemon juice added to prevent discoloration. Cook in simmering salted water until tender but still crisp, about 12 minutes. Drain well. Fry the onion gently in the melted butter until soft but not colored, then stir in the grapes and dates.

Roll out two-thirds of the pastry and use to line an 8 inch (20 cm) shallow tart pan (flan dish). Arrange the artichokes in the pastry case, slicing them if they are large. Cover with egg slices and then top with the onion mixture, seasonings and herbs.

Roll out the reserved pastry to form a lid, damp the edges and position, pressing well together; then crimp. Make a fairly large hole in the top, decorate with pastry trimmings around the hole then glaze over all with beaten egg or milk.

Cook in a fairly hot oven (400°F, 200°C, Gas Mark 6) 35 to 40 minutes or until golden brown. Heat the cream and pour into the pie through the hole. Serve hot or cold.

Preparation time about 40 minutes
Cooking time about 40 minutes
Serves 4 to 6

GADO-GADO

3 level tablespoons shredded
  (desiccated) coconut
²⁄₃ cup (6 fl oz, 175 ml) boiling
  water
5 level tablespoons crunchy peanut
  butter
1–2 cloves garlic, crushed
¼–½ level teaspoon mild chili
  powder
1 level teaspoon soft brown sugar
1 tablespoon lemon juice
2–3 scallions (green onions, spring
  onions), trimmed and chopped
salt
12 small new potatoes, scrubbed
4 carrots, peeled and thinly sliced
3 oz (75 g) mange-tout (snow
  peas), trimmed
8 oz (250 g) cauliflower florets
½ small firm green cabbage,
  trimmed and finely shredded
2–3 hard-cooked eggs

To make the sauce, pour the boiling water over the coconut and leave for 5 minutes. Put the peanut butter into a pan with the garlic, chili powder (to taste) sugar, lemon juice and coconut mixture. Bring slowly to the boil, stirring until thickened and smooth.

Cool the sauce slightly then purée or liquidize with the scallions. Return to the pan and season with salt to taste.

Bring a large pan of salted water to the boil and cook the potatoes until just tender. Remove them with a slotted spoon and add the carrots to the same water. Blanch the carrots for 4 minutes then remove and blanch the mange-tout for 2 minutes and remove. Blanch the cauliflower for five minutes and the cabbage for 2 minutes.

As the vegetables cool sufficiently to handle, rearrange in a circular design on a round plate. First use sliced new potatoes, then carrots, mange-tout and cauliflower, ending with a pile of shredded cabbage in the center and drizzle a little of the peanut sauce overall.

Just before serving, place in a microwave on MAXIMUM (100%) for 1½ to 2 minutes to reheat. Serve at once with the rest of the sauce served separately.

Preparation time about 30 minutes
Cooking time 20 minutes
Serves 4 to 6

GARLIC MUSHROOMS

1 lb (500 g) closed cup mushrooms
or button mushrooms
¾ cup (3 oz, 75 g) butter or
margarine
3–4 cloves garlic, crushed
1 tablespoon lemon juice
salt and freshly ground black
pepper
1–2 level tablespoons freshly
chopped mixed herbs or
chopped parsley and chives
sprigs of fresh herbs
4 slices toast or 8 oz (250 g) long
grain rice, boiled

Trim and wipe the mushrooms and, if large, cut into halves or quarters. Buttons can be left whole if small.

Melt the butter in a pan and add the garlic. Cook for about a minute then add the mushrooms and cook for 3 to 5 minutes, shaking and stirring almost all the time until they are just lightly cooked.

Remove from the heat, add the lemon juice and seasonings and then toss in most of the chopped herbs. Return to the heat for about a minute to reheat. Serve alone on a small plate, on pieces of toast or on a bed of rice, sprinkled with the remaining herbs.

Preparation time about 15 minutes
Cooking time about 10 minutes
Serves 4

Variation: Stir 3 to 4 tablespoons cream, sour cream or natural yogurt through the mushrooms just before serving. Toss with freshly cooked pasta.

Green and Gold Vegetable Medley

⅓ cup (2 oz, 50 g) butter
grated rind of ¼ lemon
1 level tablespoon freshly chopped parsley
1 level teaspoon each of freshly chopped thyme and tarragon
4 oz (100 g) mange-tout (snow peas), trimmed
4 oz (100 g) French beans, trimmed
8 oz (250 g) broccoli florets
6 oz (175 g) frozen peas
4 oz (100 g) baby corn
7 oz (200 g) can or frozen sweet corn niblets
1 large yellow bell pepper (capsicum), seeded and sliced
2 tablespoons (1 oz, 25 g) butter or margarine, melted
8–12 oz (250–350 g) baby new potatoes, scraped

To make the savory butter, soften the butter then beat in the lemon rind and herbs. Form into a cylinder about 1 inch (2.5 cm) in diameter. Wrap in plastic wrap (cling film) or non-stick baking paper and chill until required.

Prepare the vegetables: Bring 2 pans of salted water to the boil. Blanch the mange-tout for 3 minutes in one pan; cook baby corn in another for 3 minutes. Drain each and add beans to one pan and cook for 3 to 4 minutes; add potatoes to the other for about 10 minutes; cook broccoli for 4 to 5 minutes. Frozen peas need 3 to 4 minutes; frozen sweet corn 3 to 4 minutes (canned sweet corn just needs reheating). Fry the bell pepper gently in the melted butter for 3 to 4 minutes.

Arrange the different types of vegetables on a flat plate alternating green vegetables with yellow ones. Finally slice the savory butter and place in the center of the vegetables and serve.

Preparation time about 30 minutes
Cooking time about 25 minutes
Serves 4 to 6

Note: The vegetables can be cooked in advance, arranged on a microwave plate (without the savory butter), covered and cooked on MAXIMUM (100%) for 2 minutes when required. Add the butter just before serving.

GREEN AND WHITE
BROCCOLI POLONAISE

1 small cauliflower
¾–1 lb (350–500 g) broccoli
salt
3 slices white bread
3–4 tablespoons (1½–2 oz,
*   40–50 g) butter or margarine*
1 hard-cooked egg
1 level tablespoon freshly chopped
*   parsley*
paprika pepper

Cut both the cauliflower and broccoli into florets. Heat 2 pans of salted water and cook the vegetables separately for about 5 minutes each until only just tender. Drain thoroughly and toss together. Turn into a warmed dish and keep warm.

Meanwhile cut off the crusts from the bread and make into breadcrumbs. Fry in the melted butter gently until golden brown, stirring all the time. Either finely grate or finely chop the egg and mix with the breadcrumbs and parsley. Spoon the crumb mixture over the vegetables and then sprinkle lightly with paprika before serving.

Preparation time about 15 minutes
Cooking time about 10 minutes
Serves 4 to 5

Variation: The broccoli and cauliflower may be tossed in 1 cup (8 fl oz, 250 ml) white sauce before adding the polonaise topping.

HOT POTATO SALAD

1½ lb (750 g) small new potatoes
salt and pepper
6 tablespoon salad oil
1 tablespoons wine vinegar
grated rind of ½ lemon
1 tablespoon lemon juice
½ level teaspoon Dijon mustard
1 level teaspoon superfine (caster)
   sugar
1 can anchovy fillets, drained and
   finely chopped
2 level tablespoons capers
4 scallions (green onions, spring
   onions) trimmed and chopped
1 level tablespoon freshly chopped
   parsley
12 black olives

Scrub the potatoes but do not scrape or peel. Cook in boiling salted water until just tender. Alternatively, place the potatoes in a covered bowl with 4 tablespoons water in a microwave on MAXIMUM (100%) for 9 to 10 minutes and stand for 8 to 10 minutes.

Make the dressing by beating together the oil, vinegar, lemon rind and juice, seasonings, mustard and sugar until emulsified then mix in the chopped anchovies, capers, scallions and half the parsley.

Drain the potatoes, cut any large ones into pieces so they are all of an even size. Add the dressing to the hot potatoes, toss thoroughly and quickly turn into a serving dish. Add the black olives and sprinkle with the remaining parsley before serving.

Preparation time about 15 minutes
Cooking time about 15 minutes
Serves 4

HOT VEGETABLE SALAD

12–16 baby onions, peeled
3–4 sticks celery
3–4 carrots (approx 8 oz, 250 g),
  peeled
1 small red bell pepper
  (capsicum), seeded and sliced
4 oz (100 g) button mushrooms,
  trimmed
4 oz (100 g) mange-tout (snow
  peas), trimmed
4 tablespoons French dressing
4 tablespoons natural yogurt
1 level tablespoon freshly chopped
  coriander or parsley

Put the onions into a fairly large pan with plenty of water, bring to the boil and simmer for about 15 minutes.

Meanwhile cut the celery and carrots into sticks about 2 inches (5 cm) long. Add these to the onions and continue cooking for 10 minutes, then add the bell pepper and cook for another 5 minutes.

Finally add the mushrooms and mange-tout, bring back to the boil and simmer for 3 to 4 minutes.

Combine the French dressing, yogurt and most of the chopped coriander. Beat until thick and smooth.

Drain the vegetables thoroughly and immediately toss in the dressing. Turn into a bowl and serve hot.

Preparation time about 20 minutes
Cooking time about 35 minutes
Serves 4 to 6

Variation: Vegetables can be substituted according to personal taste and availability. The dressing can be flavored to your taste too. Try adding blue cheese, crumbled crisply grilled bacon or finely chopped hard-cooked egg and vary the herbs to tarragon, thyme, dill or mint.

HOUMMOS WITH HOT CRUDITÉS

15 oz (425 g) can chick peas
2 cloves garlic, crushed
3 tablespoons lemon juice
1 tablespoon olive oil
4 level tablespoons tahini (sesame paste)
salt and pepper
1 level tablespoon freshly chopped parsley
2–3 carrots, peeled and cut into thick sticks
1 yellow or orange bell pepper (capsicum), seeded and sliced
1 red bell pepper (capsicum), seeded and sliced
8 oz (250 g) broccoli, cut into florets
1 bulb Florence fennel, cut into strips
3 oz (75 g) mange-tout (snow peas), trimmed

Drain the chick peas, reserving the liquid. Put into a food processor or blender with 3 tablespoons of the liquid, the garlic, lemon juice and olive oil. Purée until smooth.

Add the tahini and plenty of seasonings and purée again until smooth.

Adjust the seasonings and stir in most of the chopped parsley. Turn into a bowl, sprinkle with the rest of the parsley and cover with plastic wrap (cling film) and leave to stand for up to 2 hours, if time allows.

Prepare hot crudités when ready to serve. Blanch the vegetables in 2 pans of boiling water, putting the bell peppers in one pan and the other ingredients in the other pan. They need 2 minutes each, apart from the mange-tout which only need 1 minute. Drain very thoroughly and serve immediately to accompany the hoummos, using a fork to pick up the crudités.

Preparation time about 20 minutes
Cooking time about 10 minutes
Serves 4 to 6

LEEK AND ZUCCHINI GRATIN

3 leeks (approx 1 lb, 500 g),
*   trimmed*
salt and pepper
3 zucchini (courgettes) (¾–1 lb,
*   350–500 g) trimmed*
2–3 tablespoons (1–1½ oz,
*   25–40 g) butter or margarine*
4 tablespoons light (single) cream
*   or natural yogurt*
2 level tablespoons fresh
*   breadcrumbs*
2 level tablespoons grated
*   parmesan cheese*
2 level tablespoons very finely
*   chopped red bell pepper*
*   (capsicum), blanched*

Cut the leeks into quarters lengthwise then into lengths of approximately 2½ inches (6 cm). Blanch in boiling salted water for 2 to 3 minutes. Drain thoroughly and keep warm.

Cut the zucchini into narrow strips or thin slices and blanch for 1½ to 2 minutes and then drain thoroughly.

Melt the butter in a non-stick pan and toss in first the leeks and then the zucchini and heat for 2 to 3 minutes, shaking the pan frequently and stirring carefully to prevent them breaking up. Season well.

Turn into a flameproof dish, spoon the cream overall and then sprinkle with a mixture of crumbs and grated cheese. Place under a fairly low broiler (griller) for a few minutes until lightly browned.

Serve sprinkled with finely chopped red bell pepper (capsicum).

Preparation time about 20 minutes
Cooking time about 5 minutes
Serves 4

MUSHROOM AND SESAME STIR-FRY

1 bunch scallions (green onions,
  spring onions), trimmed and
  sliced
2 tablespoons sesame oil
8 oz (250 g) carrots, peeled and
  diced
1 red bell pepper (capsicum),
  seeded and sliced
1 green bell pepper (capsicum),
  seeded and sliced
1 yellow or orange bell pepper
  (capsicum), seeded and sliced
½ lb (250 g) button mushrooms,
  trimmed and halved or
  quartered
½ lb (250 g) zucchini
  (courgettes), trimmed and cut
  into sticks
1 tablespoon light soy sauce
1 tablespoon lemon juice
1 tablespoon clear honey
salt and pepper
6 oz (175 g) bean sprouts
1–2 tablespoons sesame seeds

Fry the scallions quickly in the heated oil for a minute
or so. Add the carrots and bell peppers and continue
cooking for 2 to 3 minutes, stirring frequently.

If the mushrooms are tiny they may be left whole
otherwise halve or quarter them and add to the pan
with the zucchini and continue to cook for 2 to
3 minutes.

Combine the soy sauce, lemon juice and honey and add
to the pan with plenty of seasonings followed by the
bean sprouts. Cook for a further 2 to 3 minutes and
then serve generously sprinkled with sesame seeds.

Preparation time 20 minutes
Cooking time about 15 minutes
Serves 4

PIPERADE

1–2 tablespoons vegetable oil
2 onions, peeled and thinly sliced
1–2 cloves garlic, crushed
1 large red bell pepper (capsicum),
　seeded and sliced
1 large green bell pepper
　(capsicum), seeded and sliced
1 large yellow or orange bell
　pepper (capsicum), seeded and
　sliced
4 oz (100 g) mushrooms, sliced
¾ lb (350 g) tomatoes, peeled and
　sliced
1 level tablespoon tomato paste
　(purée)
1 level teaspoon dried oregano or
　marjoram
salt and pepper
4–8 eggs

Heat the oil in a pan and fry the onions and garlic very gently until soft. Add the bell peppers and continue cooking until they are softened but not browned. Stir in the mushrooms, tomatoes, tomato paste, herbs and seasonings and simmer for 2 to 3 minutes.

Divide the mixture between 4 individual ovenproof dishes or place in a large shallow ovenproof dish and make hollows for the eggs.

Carefully break the eggs and add 1 to 2 eggs to the individual dishes or 4 to 8 eggs to the large one, sliding them into the hollows without breaking.

Cook in a hot oven (425°F, 220°C, Gas Mark 7) for 12 to 15 minutes or until the eggs are set to your preference. Serve immediately with crusty bread or rolls.

Preparation time about 20 minutes
Cooking time about 15 minutes
Serves 4

POTATO AND ZUCCHINI ROSTI

2 tablespoons vegetable oil
1 large onion, peeled and chopped
2 lb (1 kg) potatoes, peeled and
    coarsely grated
2 zucchini (courgette) trimmed
    and coarsely grated
salt and pepper
1/2 level teaspoon ground coriander
1 1/2–2 oz (40–50 g) gouda or
    cheddar cheese, grated
    (optional)

Heat 1 tablespoon oil in a large pan, add the onions and
fry gently until soft.

Put the grated potatoes into a bowl and mix in the
zucchini and fried onions; then season well with salt,
pepper and coriander.

Heat the remaining oil in the pan and add the potato
mixture. Cook gently, stirring occasionally for about
5 minutes then flatten down into a cake and cook until
browned underneath and almost cooked through, about
6 to 8 minutes.

Sprinkle the top of the potato cake with grated cheese,
if used, and put under a moderate broiler (griller) for
about 5 minutes or until lightly browned.

Serve the potato hot, cut into wedges.

Preparation time about 20 minutes
Cooking time about 20 minutes
Serves 4

POTATO AND PARSNIP GRATIN

1½ lb (750 g) parsnips, peeled
salt and coarsely ground black
    pepper
1 onion, peeled and chopped
2 tablespoons (1 oz, 25 g) butter or
    margarine
1½ lb (750 g) potatoes, peeled
¾ cup (6 fl oz, 175 ml) stock
2 oz (50 g) edam or gouda cheese,
    grated
freshly chopped coriander or
    parsley to garnish

Coarsely grate the parsnips, put into a pan, add a pinch of salt and cover with water. Bring to the boil for 2 minutes, then drain thoroughly.

Fry the onion gently in the melted butter until soft but not colored. Add to the parsnips.

Grate the potatoes coarsely, mix with the parsnips together with the stock and plenty of seasonings.

Turn the vegetables into a well-greased ovenproof dish (not too deep) and level the top. Cover with greased foil or a lid and cook in a fairly hot oven (400°F, 200°C, Gas Mark 6) for an hour.

Remove the foil and sprinkle with cheese. Return to the oven, uncovered, for 20 to 30 minutes until golden brown. Serve sprinkled with coriander or parsley.

Preparation time about 20 minutes
Cooking time 1½ hours
Serves 4

POTATO GALETTE WITH CHIVES

6 large baking potatoes (2½ lb,
   1.2 kg)
3 oz (75 g) butter
3 onions, peeled and thinly sliced
2 oz (50 g) bacon rashers, derinded
   and chopped (optional)
salt and pepper
good pinch of ground nutmeg or
   mace
3–4 level tablespoons freshly
   chopped chives

Bake the potatoes in a hot oven (425°F, 220°C, Gas Mark 7), after pricking well, for 1 to 1¼ hours until soft. Cool slightly. Split the potatoes open and scoop out the flesh.

Melt 2 tablespoons (1 oz, 25 g) butter and fry the onions and bacon (if used) very gently and only until barely colored — this should take about 10 minutes.

Mash the potato flesh adding seasonings, nutmeg and half the chives.

Add the remaining butter to the onions in the pan and when melted add the mashed potato mixture, stir thoroughly to combine, then flatten out to form a cake. Cook the potato cake on a gentle heat for 5 to 6 minutes until browned underneath.

Place under a moderate broiler (griller) in the pan, until browned on top.

Carefully slide the galette onto a serving plate and sprinkle with the remaining chives. Serve hot cut into wedges.

Preparation time about 20 minutes
Cooking time about 1 hour plus 20 to 25 minutes
Serves 4 to 6

PUMPKIN GRATIN

2–2½ lb (1–1.2 kg) pumpkin,
    peeled, seeded and chopped
    roughly
salt and pepper
1 large onion, peeled and thinly
    sliced
1–2 tablespoons vegetable oil
2 level teaspoons freshly chopped
    thyme or 1 level teaspoon dried
    thyme
2–4 level tablespoons natural
    yogurt
2 level tablespoons parmesan
    cheese, grated

Cook the pumpkin in boiling salted water until tender, about 20 minutes; or alternatively steam it for about 30 minutes until tender. Drain well.

Meanwhile fry the onion gently in the oil until soft but only just beginning to color then stir in the thyme.

Mash the pumpkin either using a potato masher or a food processor and beat in the yogurt to give the desired consistency, then season to taste.

Turn the pumpkin purée into an ovenproof dish and spread the onion mixture over it; then sprinkle with the cheese.

Cook in a moderately hot oven (375°F, 190°C, Gas Mark 5) for about 20 minutes until the cheese is browned.

Preparation time about 25 minutes
Cooking time about 20 minutes
Serves 4 to 5

QUICK TOMATO, MUSHROOM AND OLIVE PIZZA

2 cups (8 oz, 250 g) self-rising (self-raising) flour

¼ cup (2 oz, 50 g) butter or margarine

salt and pepper

1 level teaspoon dried oregano

1 egg, beaten

3 tablespoons milk or skimmed milk

1–2 cloves garlic, crushed

1 large onion, peeled and chopped

1 tablespoon vegetable oil

1 lb (500 g) tomatoes, peeled and sliced or a 15 oz (425 g) can peeled tomatoes, partly drained and sliced

2 level tablespoons tomato paste (purée)

½ teaspoon Worcestershire sauce

4 oz (100 g) button mushrooms, sliced

1 can anchovy fillets, drained (optional)

10–12 black olives, halved and stoned

2 oz (50 g) cheddar or mozarella cheese

Sift the flour into a bowl and rub in the butter finely. Add a pinch of salt and pepper and the oregano; then add the egg and sufficient milk to mix to a fairly soft but manageable dough. Pat out the dough on a floured surface to a round of approx ¾ inch (2 cm) thick and 8–9 inches (20–23 cm) in diameter. Transfer to a well-floured or greased baking sheet.

Fry the garlic and onion in the oil until soft. Add the tomatoes, tomato paste, Worcestershire sauce and seasonings and cook for about 5 minutes until soft. Add the mushrooms and continue for 1 to 2 minutes.

Spread the tomato mixture over the scone base and arrange a lattice of anchovy fillets over it. Dot with pieces of olive and either sprinkle with grated cheddar or arrange slices of mozarella over all.

Cook in a fairly hot oven (400°F, 200°C, Gas Mark 6) for 30 to 40 minutes until firm and the cheese has browned. Serve hot or cold.

Preparation time about 20 minutes
Cooking time about 40 minutes
Serves 4 to 5

SCALLOPED POTATOES WITH BACON AND TARRAGON

2 lb (1 kg) potatoes
salt and pepper
1 large onion, peeled and finely
*   chopped*
1 level tablespoon finely chopped
*   tarragon or 1 level teaspoon*
*   dried tarragon*
3 oz (75 g) bacon rashers, derinded
*   and chopped*
1 cup (8 fl oz, 250 ml) light
*   (single) cream or milk*
2 oz (50 g) mature cheddar or
*   gruyère cheese, grated*
fresh tarragon or parsley to
*   garnish*

Peel and dice the potatoes. Place half in a greased ovenproof casserole and season well. Sprinkle with the onion, tarragon and bacon then cover with the rest of the potatoes, leveling the top as much as possible.

Pour the cream over the potatoes and cover with a piece of greased foil. Cook in a fairly hot oven (400°F, 200°C, Gas Mark 6) for 1¼ to 1½ hours or until almost tender.

Remove the foil and sprinkle the potatoes with cheese. Return to the oven, uncovered, for 15 to 20 minutes until lightly browned. Serve hot garnished with fresh tarragon or parsley. Alternatively, place in a microwave and cover and cook on MAXIMUM (100%) for 10 to 12 minutes; then brown under broiler (griller).

Preparation time about 15 minutes
Cooking time 1½–1¾ hours
Serves 4

Variation: The potatoes may be sliced, if preferred. Simply layer up half, add the other ingredients and top with the remaining sliced potatoes making an attractive design on top.

Health tip: Use stock in place of the cream or milk to reduce the calories.

SPICED OKRA

2 large onions, peeled
3 tablespoons (1½ oz, 40 g)
    butter or margarine
3–4 cloves garlic, crushed
salt and black pepper
2 level teaspoons ground coriander
½ level teaspoon turmeric
1 lb (500 g) okra (ladies fingers)
8 oz (250 g) can tomatoes
1 level teaspoon freshly chopped
    mint or ½ level teaspoon dried
    mint
2 level teaspoons tomato paste
    (purée)
½ level teaspoon garam masala

Slice one of the onions and fry in the melted butter until soft.

Liquidize or mince the other onion with the garlic and add to the pan with plenty of salt and pepper, the coriander and turmeric and cook gently for 5 minutes, stirring from time to time.

Top and tail the okra and cut into ½ inch (1 cm) pieces, add to the pan and mix thoroughly. Cover the pan and simmer very gently for 20 minutes.

Add the canned tomatoes, mint, tomato paste and garam masala and continue to simmer gently for 10 to 15 minutes, stirring occasionally.

Adjust the seasonings and serve hot with boiled rice and papadums or as an accompaniment to other curry dishes.

Preparation time about 15 minutes
Cooking time about 45 minutes
Serves 4

SPICED RED CABBAGE

1 tablespoon vegetable oil
1 small onion, peeled and finely
  chopped
1½ lb (750 g) red cabbage,
  trimmed and finely shredded
salt and pepper
2 tablespoons wine vinegar
1 level tablespoon brown sugar
1 small dessert apple, peeled, cored
  and chopped
2–3 tablespoons water

Heat the oil in a flameproof casserole and fry the onion gently until soft but not colored.

Add the cabbage and mix well, then season with salt and pepper. Add the vinegar, sugar, apple and water and bring to the boil, stirring frequently.

Cover the casserole tightly and cook in a moderate oven (350°F, 180°C, Gas Mark 4) for an hour. Stir well before serving piping hot. Alternatively, place in a microwave on MAXIMUM (100%) for 4 minutes; stir well and cook a further 4 to 5 minutes.

Preparation time about 15 minutes
Cooking time about an hour
Serves 4 to 6

Note: The cabbage is even better if cooked earlier in the day and then reheated in a moderate oven for about 20 minutes before serving.

SPINACH AND CHEESE PHYLLO PARCELS

*12 oz (350 g) fresh Swiss chard
  (spinach)*
salt and pepper
4 oz (100 g) cottage cheese
*3 oz (75 g) mature cheddar cheese,
  grated*
1 egg, beaten
small amount powdered garlic
good dash of Worcestershire sauce
¼ level teaspoon ground coriander
8 sheets phyllo pastry
*2 tablespoons (1 oz, 25 g) butter,
  melted*

Trim the Swiss chard (spinach), wash thoroughly and put into a pan. Add a little boiling water and a pinch of salt and cook until very tender.

Beat the cottage cheese, cheddar, egg, garlic, Worcestershire sauce and coriander together in a bowl.

Drain the Swiss chard (spinach) thoroughly using a potato masher to remove all the water, cool a little then chop finely and beat into the cheese mixture.

Spread out the sheets of phyllo pastry and brush each lightly with melted butter.

Divide the filling into 8 and spread one portion over about ⅛ of each piece of pastry at one end leaving a pastry margin each side. Fold over the margins to cover the edge of the filling and then fold up to make a parcel. Stand the parcels on a greased baking sheet and brush with the remaining butter.

Cook in a fairly hot oven (400°F, 200°C, Gas Mark 6) for about 20 minutes or until a light golden brown and crisp. Serve hot or cold.

Preparation time about 20 minutes
Cooking time about 20 minutes
Serves 4

SPINACH AND CHEESE SOUFFLÉ

*8oz (250 g) fresh trimmed Swiss
    chard (spinach), washed
12 oz (350 g) cottage cheese
2 level tablespoons grated
    parmesan cheese
4 eggs, separated
salt and pepper
little powdered or crushed garlic
3 tablespoons natural yogurt
4 level teaspoons powdered
    gelatine
1 tablespoon lemon juice
1 tablespoon water
lemon twists*

Prepare 4 individual soufflé dishes with paper collars tied round them using non-stick baking paper or foil.

Cook the Swiss chard (spinach) in a minimum of water for about 8 minutes until tender, then drain thoroughly and cool slightly.

Purée the Swiss chard (spinach) in a food processor or blender then add the cottage cheese and purée again.

Turn into a bowl and beat in the parmesan cheese, egg yolks, seasonings and garlic to taste, followed by the yogurt. Chill.

Dissolve the gelatine in the lemon juice and water in a small bowl over a pan of gently simmering water until clear; or in a microwave oven. Cool a little then stir evenly through the Swiss chard (spinach) mixture.

Beat the egg whites until very stiff and dry and fold through the Swiss chard (spinach) mixture evenly. Divide between the dishes and chill until set.

To serve, remove the paper or foil collars carefully and garnish each dish with a thin twisted slice of lemon.

*Preparation time about 25 minutes plus setting
Cooking time 10 minutes
Serves 4*

SPINACH ROULADE
WITH CREAM CHEESE FILLING

1 lb (500 g) frozen or 2 lb (1 kg)
  fresh Swiss chard (spinach)
  (¾ lb, 350 g) after cooking and
  draining)
3 level tablespoons natural yogurt
salt and pepper
¼ level teaspoon ground nutmeg
  or coriander
4–5 eggs, separated
1½ cups (12 oz, 350 g) cream
  cheese
½ level teaspoon garlic powder
2 level tablespoons freshly chopped
  mixed herbs
4 tablespoons natural yogurt
2 hard-cooked eggs, finely chopped

Line a jelly roll pan (swiss roll tin) 13 x 9 inches (33 × 23 cm) with non-stick baking paper.

Cook the Swiss chard (spinach) and squeeze out as much moisture as possible to give ¾ lb (350 g), then chop very finely either by hand or in a food processor.

Beat in the yogurt, seasonings, nutmeg and egg yolks until smoothly blended.

Beat the egg whites until very stiff and standing in peaks. Beat 2 tablespoons of the whites into the Swiss chard (spinach) mixture then carefully fold in the remainder evenly. Pour into the pan and spread out evenly. Cook in a fairly hot oven (400°F, 200°C, Gas Mark 6) for 15 to 20 minutes until set.

Meanwhile combine all the remaining ingredients for the filling, seasoning to taste. Turn the roulade onto a sheet of non-stick baking paper and peel off the cooking paper. Spread the cheese mixture over it quickly then roll up carefully with the help of the paper.

Transfer to a serving dish and return to the oven for a few minutes before serving cut into slices.

Preparation time about 30 minutes
Cooking time about 20 minutes
Serves 4 to 6

Stir-fried Carrots with Pineapple

1 lb (500 g) carrots, peeled and
   thinly sliced
2 tablespoons (1 oz, 25 g) butter or
   margarine
1 tablespoon vegetable oil
1 onion, peeled and finely chopped
1 clove garlic, crushed (optional)
½ inch (1.5 cm) piece fresh ginger,
   peeled and finely grated
7 oz (200 g) can pineapple in
   natural juice, chopped
2 tablespoons pineapple juice
salt and pepper
chopped dill or parsley

Blanch the carrots in boiling water for 2 minutes then drain thoroughly.

Heat the butter and oil in a heavy based pan, add the onion, garlic (if used) and ginger and cook over a brisk heat for 2 to 3 minutes until just beginning to color.

Quickly add the carrots, lower the heat and fry for about 5 minutes, stirring frequently.

Add the pineapple and juice and plenty of seasonings and continue to cook for 5 to 6 minutes until the carrots are tender-crisp.

Serve in a warmed dish sprinkled with chopped herbs.

Preparation time about 15 minutes
Cooking time about 15 minutes
Serves 4 to 5

STUFFED ZUCCHINI

4 large zucchini (courgettes)
4 oz (100 g) sliced bacon, derinded
   and chopped
1 small onion, peeled and finely
   chopped
1 clove garlic, crushed
6 oz (175 g) broccoli florets,
   chopped
salt and pepper
2 level tablespoons natural yogurt
2 level tablespoons grated
   parmesan cheese
1 level tablespoon sesame seeds
grated carrot

Cut the stalks off the zucchini and then cut them each in half lengthwise. Scoop out part of the flesh from the center of each and chop. Arrange the zucchinis in a shallow ovenproof dish in a single layer.

Fry the bacon, onion and garlic in a non-stick pan with no extra oil until the bacon fat begins to run then continue cooking until soft.

Add the chopped zucchini flesh and chopped broccoli and continue to cook for 2 to 3 minutes, stirring frequently.

Season well, stir in the yogurt and spoon into the zucchini, piling up as necessary.

Combine the parmesan and sesame seeds and sprinkle over the zucchini. Cook in a fairly hot oven (400°F, 200°C, Gas Mark 6) for about 25 minutes until the topping is lightly browned and the zucchini just tender. Alternatively, place in a microwave on MAXIMUM (100%) for 3 to 4 minutes and brown under a broiler (griller).

Serve hot. Garnish with piles of grated carrot.

Preparation time about 20 minutes
Cooking time about 25 minutes
Serves 4

VEGETABLE MACARONI BAKE

8 oz (250 g) short cut macaroni or
   other similar pasta shapes
5 tablespoons (2½ oz, 65 g)
   butter or margarine
⅓ cup (1½ oz, 40 g) flour
1¾ cups (¾ pint, 450 ml) milk or
   skimmed milk
4 oz (100 g) mature cheddar
   cheese, grated
½ level teaspoon dry mustard
salt and pepper
1–2 cloves garlic, crushed
3 carrots, peeled and diced
1 red bell pepper (capsicum),
   seeded and sliced
2 zucchini (courgettes), trimmed
   and thinly sliced
4 oz (100 g) mushrooms, sliced
1 level tablespoon tomato paste
   (purée)
½ level teaspoon dried oregano

Cook the macaroni until barely tender in boiling water, drain immediately and rinse.

Melt 3 tablespoons (1½ oz, 40 g) butter in a pan, stir in the flour and cook for a minute or so. Gradually add the milk and bring to the boil, stirring until thickened. Stir in just over half the cheese, the mustard and seasonings to taste.

Melt the remaining butter and add the garlic and carrots. Fry gently for 3 to 4 minutes then add the red bell pepper and continue to cook for 2 minutes. Add the zucchini, mushrooms, seasonings, tomato paste and herbs and cook for 1 to 2 minutes.

Put half the macaroni in a greased ovenproof dish and cover with the vegetable mixture. Add about a third of the sauce then add the rest of the macaroni and the rest of the sauce.

Sprinkle with the remaining cheese and cook in a fairly hot oven (400°F, 200°C, Gas Mark 6) for 30 to 40 minutes until bubbling and brown. Serve hot. Alternatively, place in a microwave on MAXIMUM (100%) for 5 minutes, then brown under the broiler (griller).

Preparation time about 30 minutes
Cooking time about 40 minutes
Serves 4

VEGETABLE MOUSSAKA

2 eggplants (aubergines) (approx
   1½ lb, 750 g), trimmed
salt and pepper
2 onions, peeled and thinly sliced
2 tablespoons vegetable oil
1–2 cloves garlic, crushed
1 lb (500 g) tomatoes, sliced
1 level tablespoon tomato paste
   (purée)
1 level teaspoon dried basil
4 oz (100 g) mushrooms, sliced
1 lb (500 g) potatoes, peeled and
   parboiled
2 eggs
⅔ cup (5 fl oz, 150 ml) natural
   yogurt
2 tablespoons milk
1½ oz (40 g) cheddar cheese,
   grated (optional)
chopped parsley

Slice the eggplants about ¾ inch (2 cm) thick and sprinkle liberally with salt; leave for 20 minutes then rinse off the salt from the slices and drain thoroughly.

Meanwhile fry the onions gently in the oil until soft but not colored, about 10 minutes, then add the garlic, tomatoes, tomato paste, basil, seasonings and 3 tablespoons water and cook gently for 3 to 4 minutes. Add the mushrooms and seasonings and continue to cook for 3 to 4 minutes.

Arrange half the eggplant slices in a greased ovenproof casserole and cover with half the tomato mixture. Add the potatoes diced or sliced in an even layer then top with the rest of the tomato mixture and eggplants.

Cover with greased foil and cook in a moderate oven (350°F, 180°C, Gas Mark 4) for 40 minutes.

Beat the eggs and yogurt together then beat in the milk and seasonings and spoon over the eggplants. Sprinkle with the cheese, and return to the oven, uncovered, for about 20 minutes or until the custard is lightly set and browned. Serve sprinkled with parsley.

Preparation time about 30 minutes
Cooking time about an hour
Serves 4 to 6

VEGETABLE SAMOSAS

1 tablespoon vegetable oil
1 onion, peeled and finely chopped
1 clove garlic, crushed
1 red bell pepper (capsicum),
*   seeded and chopped*
2 carrots, peeled and coarsely
*   grated*
1 boiled potato, finely chopped
¾ cup (4 oz, 100 g) cooked peas
1 level teaspoon garam masala
1–2 level teaspoons Madras curry
*   powder*
salt and pepper
2 cups (8 oz, 250 g) self rising
*   (self-raising) flour*
2 tablespoons (1 oz, 25 g) butter
cold water to mix
vegetable oil for cooking
½ cup (4 oz, 125 ml) thick set
*   natural yogurt or Greek yogurt*
1 level tablespoon very finely
*   chopped onion (extra)*
2 level tablespoons mango
*   chutney, chopped*
1 level tablespoon freshly chopped
*   mint or parsley*

Heat the oil and fry the onion, garlic and bell pepper gently for about 5 minutes. Stir in the carrot and continue cooking for 2 to 3 minutes, stirring frequently.

Turn into a bowl and mix with the potato, peas, garam masala, curry powder and seasonings to taste. Leave to cool.

To make the pastry, sift the flour with a pinch of salt into a bowl and rub in the butter finely. Add sufficient water to mix to a soft but manageable dough and roll out to about ⅛ inch (3 mm) thick.

Cut into 3 inch (7.5 cm) rounds. Put 2 teaspoons of the filling on each round, fold over the pastry, damp the edges with water and press well together.

Fry in hot deep oil, a few at a time, until golden brown. Drain on paper towels. Combine all the remaining ingredients for the sauce and serve with the samosas garnished with tomato wedges and watercress.

Preparation time about 35 to 40 minutes
Cooking time about 15 minutes
Serves 4

VEGETARIAN STIR-FRY

1 large onion, peeled and thinly
*   sliced*
2 tablespoons sesame or walnut oil
4 sticks celery, thinly sliced
8 oz (250 g) carrots, peeled and
*   cut into sticks*
2–4 oz (50–100 g) pecan or walnut
*   halves*
1 red bell pepper (capsicum),
*   seeded and cut into strips*
8–12 oz (250–350 g) zucchini,
*   trimmed and thinly sliced*
1–1½ lb (500-750 g) white
*   cabbage, finely shredded*
4 oz (100 g) stoned dates, halved
salt and pepper
1 tablespoon lemon juice
freshly chopped parsley

Fry the onion briskly in the oil until beginning to color. Add the celery and carrots and continue cooking for 3 to 4 minutes, stirring from time to time.

Stir in the pecans or walnuts, bell pepper and zucchini and fry, stirring almost all the time for 3 to 4 minutes.

Add the cabbage and dates and continue to cook for 3 to 4 minutes.

Season well and add the lemon juice. Heat through thoroughly and serve in a warmed dish liberally sprinkled with parsley.

Preparation time 20 minutes
Cooking time about 15 minutes
Serves 4

Zucchini and Tarragon Quiches

2 zucchini (courgettes) (12 oz, 350 g), trimmed
1½ cups (6 oz, 175 g) all purpose (plain) flour or malted wheat flour
salt and pepper
3 tablespoons (1½ oz, 40 g) butter or margarine
3 tablespoons (1½ oz, 40 g) lard
cold water to mix
6 scallions (green onions, spring onions), trimmed and sliced
2 level tablespoons freshly chopped tarragon or 1 level tablespoon dried tarragon
2 eggs
½ cup (4 fl oz, 100 ml) light (single) or sour cream
½ cup (4 fl oz, 100 ml) milk

Coarsely grate the zucchini and place in a bowl. Cover liberally with boiling water, stir well and let stand for 5 minutes.

Sift the white flour and a pinch of salt into a bowl (do not sift the malted wheat flour) then rub in the butter and lard until the mixture resembles fine breadcrumbs. Add sufficient water to mix to a pliable dough.

Roll out the pastry on a lightly floured surface and use to line 6 individual tart pans or Yorkshire pudding tins 4½ inches (11 cm) in diameter.

Drain the zucchini very thoroughly using a potato masher to extract the maximum water. Mix with the scallions and divide between the pastry cases; sprinkle with the tarragon.

Beat the eggs with plenty of seasonings and the cream and milk. Spoon into the pastry and cook in a fairly hot oven (400°F, 200°C, Gas Mark 6) for 25 to 30 minutes. Serve hot or cold.

Preparation time 20 minutes
Cooking time about 30 minutes
Serves 6

Health tip: Replace the cream with milk or skimmed milk to reduce the calories.

ZUCCHINI AND TOMATO TIAN

*1 large or 2 smaller onions, peeled
   and sliced*
1 tablespoon vegetable oil
1–2 cloves garlic, crushed
*1½ lb (750 g) zucchini
   (courgettes), trimmed and
   sliced*
*1 lb (500 g) tomatoes, peeled and
   sliced*
*2 level tablespoons freshly chopped
   basil or 1 level tablespoon dried
   basil*
salt and pepper
3 tablespoons dry white wine
*1 level tablespoon tomato paste
   (purée)*
2 level tablespoons breadcrumbs
*2 level tablespoons grated
   parmesan cheese*

Fry the onions in the oil for 5 to 10 minutes then add the garlic and continue cooking for 2 to 3 minutes.

In a greased ovenproof dish layer up the zucchini, onions and tomatoes to give 2 to 3 layers of each, finishing with tomatoes; season and sprinkle with chopped herbs as you layer.

Combine the wine and tomato paste and pour over all. Cover the casserole with a lid of foil.

Cook in a fairly hot oven (400°F, 200°C, Gas Mark 6) for 45 minutes. Remove the lid, combine the breadcrumbs and parmesan and sprinkle over the top. Place under a moderate broiler (griller) for a few minutes until the topping is browned. Alternatively, place in a microwave on MAXIMUM (100%) for 5 minutes, stand for 5 minutes then cook a further 5 minutes; brown under a broiler (griller).

Serve hot or cold garnished with sprigs of basil.

Preparation time 15 to 20 minutes
Cooking time about 50 minutes
Serves 4 to 6

INDEX

An illustration for each recipe appears opposite the listed page.